Face It

BY THE SAME AUTHOR

Enchant / Extinguish

M. Stasiak

Face It

Shearsman Books

First published in the United Kingdom in 2026 by
Shearsman Books
P.O. Box 4239
Swindon
SN3 9FN

Shearsman Books Ltd Registered Office
30–31 St. James Place, Mangotsfield, Bristol BS16 9JB
(this address not for correspondence)

EU AUTHORISED REPRESENTATIVE:
Lightning Source France
1 Av. Johannes Gutenberg, 78310 Maurepas, France
Email: compliance@lightningsource.fr

www.shearsman.com

ISBN 978-1-83738-018-3

Copyright © M. Stasiak, 2026

The right of M. Stasiak to be identified as the author
of this work has been asserted by her in accordance with the
Copyrights, Designs and Patents Act of 1988.
All rights reserved.

Contents

SLIP INTO HACKNEY

Slip into Hackney	9
This is the truth	12
Made and made over	13
Hackney Brook	15
The end of the estate	16
Bringing back the light	17
donna & lucy & all the rest	19
To be a dead thing	21
dog, woman	22
The promise	24
Rosary	25
Nine stops	26
Bracelet	31
In which I rest	33
In August it was too hot	34

PERSEPHONE'S FIELD

Persephone's field	37
Mothered	39
Fathered	40
Inducted	41
Aeons	42
Pomegranate	43
Go back	44
Emerging	45
Home	46
Obsidian's cousin	47

CLOSING FOCUS

Closing focus	51
Re/wilding	53
Seen through glass	54
The verge	56

RECKONING

Surety	61
#Bring your true self to work	63
Reckoning	65
Befriend it again	66
Room 13	67
Face it	68
When all else ends	69

FREE WILL

Free will	73

Notes	88
Acknowledgements	89

SLIP INTO HACKNEY

Slip into Hackney

Slip into Hackney, over your head.
Pass under, between, beside, beyond and through.

You've made a choice to trust your weight to
Hackney's streets and surfaces

so let the place take you.

Part the people crowding the thoroughfare.
There's been an infinity.

Ease apart the assemblage of the city.
Set it aside.

The clay gouged out and shuttered into moulds,
and baked and stacked and turned to rooms for people
      can be returned to earth.

The earth dug out for wires and lines and drains,
restrained and changed and mixed with other substances,
      can be restored and simplified, undone.

The roads can be unmade again.
The fields can be undug again.
The people lie unmarked and unrecalled.

Wander the woodland far before
a place you know the name for.

Wander the woodland somewhere near
a marsh, a stream, the sound of geese.

Become another, other, any living thing.

There's time for you.

Allow yourself

those long uncounted centuries
of rest.

This is the physical world
that built you and birthed you,
wrapped you in substance,
set you in life.

It's with you to the end.

But be aware.

The air is full of energy.
The planet's full of energy.
You can't escape – there's heat inside
the centre of your bones, and
somewhere out in time there's
movement
agile and alive.
It calls for you.

Come back now.
Come back to now.
Hackney is urgent, needing you here.

This is the truth

There really was a weary pair of guards, who may have been in wines and beers or may have been in household goods, and also Mr Crouch who with a friend or on his own said simply or simply didn't say *I bet those twats won't see*, who did or didn't go there through the wind because he thought he recognised a mate. The lights of evening *Kwikshop* shone through glass, on rain and coats and cars and chasing through the gloom our man here certainly got jumped (whether Dilan showed the right ID or not, whoever had him by whichever arms and legs). It's true they dragged him in by Aisle 1, after the bottle fell or didn't from his coat, after his flailing fist hit Duncan in the mouth, which may have bled or may have merely bruised, and the police came after someone (Kenny?) called. I can confirm that things were said, that fighting could have finished with a kicking in the balls, or maybe when he figured out the odds, and cameras caught it all although the tape – before it disappeared at least – was clearly blank. And it's gospel: after everyone was gone a weary cleaner swept up broken glass, or it was kicked along by several strangers' feet, into the dark.

Made and made over

every surface
                    made and made over

Victorians
                    dragging whole neighbourhoods out of fields

philanthropists
                    heaping poverty in dense blocks

no homes for heroes in these caustic streets

cemeteries of addresses
                    shaded on black maps

a raw wind billowing concrete
                    down staircases, into yards

and suddenly you at 8, pausing skinny as a whippet

compass point scratching your name

fleet-footing it
                    through 60s towers and 70s blank walls

through decades of pvc and chrome

slipping
                    into a mirrored millennium

every surface
                    made and made over

    your scuffs and scratches
                        veiled now

    under deeper cuts and darker crimes

    your feet
             that kept the pavements turning, kept

    gravity in place
                    now trod and trod away   noiseless

    into a brave new

    reckless
            shiney sold-out world

Hackney Brook

What did they do with our
Hackney Brook? Tidied it away.

They cased it in concrete and
made it serve sewers. They filled in
the hoofprints of cattle in mud.

What will they do with our
wisdom? Chase it all away.

To fit us for working
glib and quiescent, neat inside
certainties, perjured and priced.

Marshall the cowshit and gather
your inarticulate soul.

They are pulling the leaves
off the trees in Parliament
rather than let them fall.

The end of the estate

Nakedness. Fully clothed in a bare room
woodchip painted
bold colours, terracotta concrete underfoot.

This emptiness is mine, and all the things
that fill it – space
between cracked ceiling and cracked floor

traffic on the Seven Sisters Road
and light approaching
tentative through rippled glass.

Faithlessness. Beyond the birches blocks
chased down
by money, worn out by neglect

are forced to rubble heaps, surrender
modest hopes of home
among the dirt of demolition.

Sirens rake the room, rebound against
this moment
to a future where I'm gone

and this is done, and there is just
a single magpie
scanning debris, dust and sun.

Bringing back the light

I have Roller-mouse   Saturnus keyboard
     symbols of a minor
                                work-induced
malaise.

Distraction   running angry to my fingertips
looking for out.

I have office-friendly plants   a window
turquoise double-glazed

and my stare fighting through it
desperate
          to see you on the street.

I have a phone that flashes orange   a black-
edged invitation to a church.

                  Fluorescent strips
forget me   dip to disregard

and I must wave at them
          to bring back the light

to subdue the days of pneumonia

the slope and
     clutch of the whole city

     remembering
how you walked in it   through the griefs
unguarded in your skin

as I walked in it   under the flyovers
beyond the orange lamps

moth-trailing towards remorse.

I remember rain
across our hands   mute words
      inside my mouth

how we were cradled by tower blocks,
                                      circled
by train lines at 3 a.m.

I see again the eclipse-light of hospitals
the shadowing of your face.

donna & lucy & all the rest

I saw them first on Springfield Road, tagging each other
up the hill. In leopard coat and black suede boots,
in army jacket, studded belt, they occupied the street
like it was habitat.

Later I met them at the Cricketers, with friends of
friends, a flatmate's cousin, someone's younger sister
and men in t-shirts the colour of dust.

> *Hackney: find them all and take them in,*
> *those who flow to the city.*
> *Give them homes amid uncertainty,*
> *room to find and lose themselves and*
> *find and lose each other and the world.*

They ran from childhood and claimed their lives, then
ran for London and claimed that too. They moved around
the squats and cash-in-hand and signing on, and never
talked of 'Peterborough' or 'Milton Keynes' or 'home'.

> *Hackney: put your hand around them. Blow*
> *wind between your fingers,*
> *bring debris and dust to hide and*
> *disguise them and let them slip away,*
> *beyond the reach of judgement.*

Every door that opened was inviting, they were present
in the world and free and bright. Sure they knew
the score, knew bad things happened in closed rooms.
Sure they drank too much, talked bullshit, got in fights.

> *Hackney: look after them.*
> *Stay present in the pieces of their lives.*
> *Wash streetlight into morning as they pass.*
> *Wrap night-time round their leaving as they gutter into dark.*

Chaos drew them in and chaos threw them out again. They disappeared or overdosed, were chased away, became confused, confined themselves in anxious lonely bedsits over takeaways and bars.

> *Hackney: remember them, when the next generation inherits the street, when hopefulness and heat release from concrete to another hectic evening, under another crescent moon.*

Remember them as you yourself are whispered into dusk: how they were young and they were loyal and exuberant and did their best. Remember how they flamed and flared in generosity and ash. Remember the generosity. Stay warmed by the orange flame.

To be a dead thing

Last night, home, it felt best
to be a dead thing, blown
from the tossing street
and not a creature crept here
through a crush of years
and the hardness of the last
week. Best to keep company
with wind and black chill
tamp down among this winter
and be waste and sleep well.

dog, woman

```
(i)                             (ii)
tan & white                     escalator
              dog                              down
girl dog                                handrail
              pit bull          held
head down                                      borne down
scarf         navy              below
      collar                                   figures
rope lead                       tiled
trailing                                       floor
              floor             green
rocking, moving                 camouflage jacket
              dog's                     curled
head low                        nose
      legs shaking                      to tail
tail          down              dog, tan & white
steps forward                                  pit bull
stops         nose              pink           collar
touches   woman's               scarred
knee
                                        nose
              still now          asleep        adjacent
              woman                     woman
tumbled in                      curled
      dropped                   navy bomber
rope lead     slid                             jeans
down corner                     trainers
              wordless                         scuffed
dog   stops                     asleep
              stays                     borne   down
broad head down                 floating down
stops                           stepping off
doors slide                                    continual
```

```
                to side        borne           down
open    behind                          stepping
                ahead          left at          dog
        dog     stops          for eastbound
leans forward                           right
legs            trembling      at woman         westbound
        leans in                        floating
                slowly         down
broad head                              tan & white
        laid                                    dog
between         woman's        girl dog
        knees   chest                   asleep
still except                   woman            asleep
                trembling      floating
stops                                           down
                still          stepping         left
stops                                   right
tan & white     dog                             leaving
                stays          asleep
stops                                           leaving
```

The promise

You were sweated into this basement out of dirty city walls
                      and offered everything by art.

Adrenaline-splash across the brickwork.

And then all of it sluiced away.

The city glanced
                but shook its head at riches or respect

as cigarette in hand you saw
                a lottery's-worth of luck and money
     delivered elsewhere

a random requisitioning of your entitlement.

Shutter the light
              with wooden blinds and blame.

Draw caricatures:
              an alien, an ant.

Rosary

Rain will help

so if you need to
drag me to the street
and let the water
wear away my skin

until the vast starry dark inside
mixes with
the streetlight and the noise

in wet air

then everything will be sweet.

Nine stops

*Stop 1: Finsbury Park, at which I
climb on dazed and mindless, take
a seat and others join the train.*

"This train's so dirty it's terrible
really." The lady sat down next
to me: an older person with a cane,
her shoulder-length white hair
brushing an ivory silk blouse, her
ankles crossed beneath a pale
green linen skirt. Her companion
on the other side said nothing
and subsequently nor did she.

*Stop 2: Highbury and Islington, at which
I ponder her statement and speculate about
her life.*

It was dirty it was terrible, but how?
Terrible for her, that she should have
to travel in this way – far from the
chauffeured car and country home and
expectations of her youth? Was she
feeling bad for me, or those like me who
knew no better? Was the offence to
Britain, to the ancient city of London
which isn't what it used to be? Or
was the sadness her companion – the
sighs, the silences, the failing through
the years to put things right, to buy
the mews when property was cheap,
make partner, make those changes he
had promised on their wedding day?

*Stop 3: King's Cross, at which I enter
Zone 1 and think like a civil servant.*

The state of things was understandable. Lockdown confounded the business plan while trains still poured down platforms bare of customers. I imagined stressed accountants' meetings, bargaining with government, analysis of corners to be cut while still maintaining standards of proper service and defending, while more than usually vulnerable, against the designs of disaster capitalist MPs.

*Stop 4: Euston, at which I feel empathy
for the cleaners.*

Probably outsourced, and probably immigrants, and probably working several jobs, and possibly mourning colleagues lost to Covid, and possibly ill themselves, and possibly struggling in regardless from outer boroughs, and surely underpaid but knowing their own worth if nobody else does.

*Stop 5: Warren Street, at which for the first
time I evaluate the truth of her statement.*

It wasn't dirty anyway! – no stains unwashed, no dust unswept, no coffee making patterns on the floor. I scanned for graffiti but even etched on dim distorting windows there was none, and neither was there

chocolate crushed onto the blue velour.
Everything was just a little worn –
fabric faded, kickboards flashing
silver through the black, lino slightly
scuffed and ricked and ruched.
It was just old. It had just aged,
just like the lady, just like me and
just like her inscrutable companion.

*Stop 6: Oxford Circus, at which I consider
the underground and get metaphysical.*

I thought how trains come out of
nowhere and the dark, emerge from
mystery unquestioning as dogs,
I thought of them set running from
a place I'll never see, how nothing
stops, how they go on and on and
on, keep working through the years
approaching through the earth to
take us home or out or where we
need to go, headlights roaring out
of darkness minute after minute
in the morning or late at night and
welcome after chill streets and
all our night's experience, where
bathed in the still and infinite
tomblike silence of the tunnels
we wait inside the womb of under
London, within the centuries of
settlement and bone from which
miraculous are manifested trains.

*Stop 7: Green Park, at which I become
sentimental about the nobility of
manufacturing and the emotional power
of endurance.*

I thought of their squat familiar
friendly shape, and who might
have designed them, and who
might have built them, and who
might maintain them and how
they have outlasted marriages
and governments and lives.

*Stop 8: Victoria, at which I feel
generously benign towards my
fellow travellers.*

They laboured to their feet,
the lady and her reticent
companion, stepped towards
the doors and left the train.
I wished them mutely well.
I wished them lots of other
days that didn't disappoint.

*Stop 9: Pimlico, at which I arise
and alight.*

I feel refreshed. I feel I've had a rest.
I've been in transit, in another's hands,
my only job to board the train and
be a passenger. My boot-heel hits
the floor in perfect mastery and I'm
away, striding to the exit and my day.
I've been an item moved, transported,

registered, complete. I've been
through tunnels, been in other lives.
It's been a privilege. It's been a ride.

Bracelet

Elaborate and unacceptable questions roll across my mind
increasingly ornate
like the carnellian beads from a broken bracelet

nudging round my ox-blood boots, travelling
the grooved and dusty floor.
Could your little girl stop screaming? Is it

possible, do you think, for your child to stop screaming?
Is there something wrong with her? – I mean,
I mean if she is

neuro-diverse, or in pain, or possessed
by unshakeable anguish, or even just really
enjoying herself, it is of course ok, it's fine, but otherwise…?

I'm on the 106, and just past Queen's Parade,
top deck, the left-hand side and four rows back. The girl
is right in front of me.

My hand hurts, the crimson scratch where I
cut myself earlier.
I am happy to be buried in my black astrakhan coat.

Outside the red light jolts along the road again,
unfolding into vacancy and space.
Trees observe our passing.

The girl's scarf flicks maroon across the seat back and I
can see her open mouth
but cannot any longer hear the scream, weaving

through tail-lights as I press cold fingers to my eyes and
see the night expand and fade vermilion.
Her dad looks down and smiles

and takes her red-gloved hand. Her mouth still screams.
It is ok. We are, all of us and
everything, bound into the city on a bus.

In which I rest

With sun on the soles of my feet, sun sore on my
scuffed feet, sun sore in my soul I lie fatigued and
foetal in the heart of London, laid down now because I
stood in the street before dawn, amid sirens, screams
and flashing lights and spoke with the police, and
all was torn and chaos for a while, and someone died.

It was no-one that I know, and I still don't know how
to honour them, except by lying here and letting the
exhaustion and the fact of it wash through, and
finally closing my eyes, replaying how the vehicles
went away and then the street flowed clean and empty
and the palest light began, and small birds sang.

In August it was too hot

I fell asleep across my bed, and while I slept the
sun moved over me and kept me in a dream, and I
dreamed Peter was sitting there, very quiet on
the bed alongside, and I dreamed I was in a crypt
of old grey stone with an old film running of a huge
hall, with beds in ranks and a single bucket at the
end of each row for piss & shit, but no one there.
And I woke up feeling dazed and very calm.

I didn't know the film so I could only google Peter,
to see what had become of him. I found he'd been
assistant chief then chief exec in local authorities;
had run his own consultancy for seven years; had
advised the Caymanese on administrative efficiency;
had led a Clinical Commissioning Group through
a time of crisis; and been seconded in to run
the long-awaited merger of three colleges to one.

I drifted from my kitchen to the balcony, into soft air
cascading through the rowan tree, brick and stone
beyond it and a cloud-streaked sky. Behind my eyes
had lodged a war and burned-out weaponry, and
blasted blocks, and tales of torture. Close by, the
grasses that arrived on last year's breeze were half
still sleek and purple, half puffed and golden brown,
having no choice but trusting wind and the future.

PERSEPHONE'S FIELD

1 Persephone's field

This is Persephone's field
the flat
        cropped grass

this is Persephone's field
open   featureless

it was lies about the wandering
the flowers and the friends

there was only
solitude

        only the types of grass
seeds splintered

gold on black earth
weight
        of less than nothing

not like gravity
circling her ankle
        surveilling
the space

trees would have

hidden her
stopped the sky following

leaves would have sheltered
        moving air

it was lies about the wandering
the flowers and the friends

truth was just her feet

attentive to the field
                truth was just

the field

noticing

2 Mothered

Her mother tries to welcome her, dress her in
jade and azure, embed her in comfort flowing
out of others and the world; yet faces in her
life loom alien out of the afternoon air.

Her mother tries to work with her, help her
make gardens out of the swampy wild; but
laying hands on weeds seems violence.
They occupy their space as sure as she does,
living in their wilderness, untouchable, complete.

Her mother tries to nurture her, fit her for joy and
presence. Persephone chokes on it, backing away,
becoming thin, translucent, fugitive; a brief
sketched outline on a pale expensive page.

3 Fathered

Her father tries to work with her, leads her
into the sealed and crowded rooms
so he can teach her how to speak.
She hears a language without bones,
without referents, hears a code of small
humiliations, words that offer no way in
for other words, a fly-trap disrespectful
language of assertion and mockery.
A language where winning the argument
means you have the truth.
And her father in his armoured charm
his handsome way was good at it.

He sold her.
He sold her for the rape.
He taught her the uses of daughters.

And her mother with her kindness,
her absolute intent to make life
nourishing and nice, was innocent
and absent. She didn't see a thing.

4 Inducted

Persephone is
a shaded loss
beneath an unforgiving sky.

This is her frontier
its grip, its thin air.
This is her stand-off

its ultimate
defeat.

Dissolution
gathers a black hole
spits out   necessity.

There is howling grinding
movement. She is

induced
inducted underground.

5 Aeons

Aeons pass, aeons of heat and
    pressure and the dark.
Here is the half-life, prickling
    with intent. Here is her own
new world. She has never
    known a place where meaning
is irrelevant. She has never
    seen life at deep vents.
She has never felt heavy,
    metal before; never met the
rare earths, the soft dense leads;
    never known how minerals
trawl her body; the way striated
    radiation cuts her through.

6 Pomegranate

She sees the seeds.
They are set before her
lambent as ruby
dangerous as sun.
They are harsh
and bright and fragile.
Too sharp too sweet
the taste of them
evokes pure pain
a residue
that will not wipe away.

But they are of
the mineral deep as well
formed in the proper dark.
Here they are
baptised in death
and pressure, here
they are of the living
and the dead.
Without ingesting them
she cannot leave
she cannot stay.

7 Go back

Go back screaming
Go back clawed and feathered
Go back stone

Go back grit-starred
Go back laughing
Strangling with snakes

Become the monster
The consequence of your acts

Travel within the fingers

Of an open fist

8 Emerging

Back on the earth's
face
she is grown
and gone strange

phasing in and out of night she
feels
the crow's glare
the crags of basalt
      rising through her feet

she holds threads
extremity
hauls
      lengths, the singing
iron core
the fragile land
and
trembling air
she raises

trees   rocks

fly to her grip

9 Home

Persephone goes home
and finds it muted, new
her mother sleepy
letting the seasons have their way
her father greyer
deals not done in rooms these days
he has become ceremonial

moving
through thresholds
she lets the door do what it will
letting her presence
sift from the air like dust

corners of the room
unswept

path
untended, her

step, her

absence gentle, soft

10 Obsidian's cousin

The surface of the earth
                            supports us
springs us
                 buoyant with messages
out of the chemical fluxing night.

Breezes haul from
                 arms of the crossroads
we never took.

Absurd existence   falls back into gravity.

The minerals acknowledge us
                 obsidian's cousin

made of the same material
joined with the same desire

and scampering over the surface
                 like phosphorus flame.

Only life
       burns up this quick

thin blue light and   then the sudden dark.

At the edges of territories
where cliffs, cranes, horizons
                 all align, hear it –

the roaring
>	strung magnetic stream
universe and moment given voice.

>	We're staggered back
>	>	in solar wind, wrapped

around by spinning time

>	dizzy, dazzled, joyous.

CLOSING FOCUS

Closing focus

Could the land want war? I wondered if the earth that now held their bodies had asserted a claim to them. Does not the field participate in the battle? What's left on the field are the fields and the invisible blood drained into the land.

A Terrible Love of War, James Hillman

Translation 1
Today I was 1.5 from this fucker of a town. According to the totality of the fighting, we were 30 minutes, and 5 times to the left in daylight hours. It did not look like battle, where the fighters stand knee-deep in the blood of 300 comrades. The exit of 4 seconds is to the arrival and everyone knows this.

From skyscrapers they are birding. Nine have armour rolling. Ours calculate. From the very unpleasant, the fly unwinds the rear. There are losses, I saw. The shoot is plus 500, minus 1.2.

In fields around are wheat crops, rotting on the vine. Small rodents have population. They eat everything – gunpowder, cigarettes, loading and unloading, tongues.

It's cold, it's getting close to zero, and the mud has all dried up. Yes, that's all.

Translation 2
I was a mile outside the fucking town all day. We barely fired, but guns acknowledged us at every hour. It was an abattoir with blood to the knees. I smelt our loss. We are full of nerves and the count of 4 between the launching and the death.

Weapons fly from the high-rise, yet the high-rise still remains. Ours are setting sights but have an inability to strike. We please nothing.

Mice multiply. They eat gunpowder, cigarettes, our boots and everything we seek to save.

It's cold, it's getting close to zero, and the mud has all dried up. Yes, that's all.

Translation 3
A town, it could have been a thousand sodding towns. The field and 18 streets and cross of tower blocks. Seized by the frontline, closing its eyes.

I saw a mouse observe the splintered chest of my cousin, holding congealing meat, and then run over his face.

It's cold, it's getting close to zero, and the mud has all dried up. Yes, that's all.

Translation 4
This place make formless, worthless.

The field is blood and rot and takes us down.

Yes, that's all.

Re/wilding

For countries facing the threat of invasion, rewilding
could provide both environmental and security benefits.
'Defensive rewilding', Brian Schmidt

We are re-wilding, re-
planting, putting birches
by the road and alder
on the river-bank.

We are re-wilding, re-
ceding, yielding, letting
swampland spread
and mud defend us.

We are re-wilding, re-
wiring, fighting, going
feral in distraught
and damaged forest.

We are re-wilding, re-
winding, grasping earth,
thieving life as leaves
whip by and rivers freeze.

Or ceasing, searched by
guns and summer breeze.

Seen through glass

Glass was the means of containing danger ... it showed things as images, as phenomena, fostering the mental operations that keep you on the other side of the glass, out of action.
A Terrible Love of War, James Hillman

> *Under the bodies the wreckage the tragedy,*
> *what goes down? Because those of us*
> *watching need to know who wins.*

Armies trade treelines, capture recapture
    50 yards of road.

Tanks detonate like fireworks.

> *The line stays still. We see only explosion,*
> *confusion, stasis, rush.*

Trenches fill with water.
    Winter wanders through.

Surveillance ruins strategies and plans.

> *We must make sense of it, explore*
> *authoritative sources.*

Resolute and delicate at night, someone
    blows up railways.

Industrial agility sinks ships.

We must grip doctrine, logistics, tactics,
the invader's soul.

Machine tools matter now.
        Ball-bearings matter now.

Someone loses power if this war ends.

The interlocking spheres are pleasing, intricate.
But do they shift the line?

Influence comes good.
        Duplicity comes good.

Constructed famine moves across the land.

Because for all this explanation,
yes yes yes —

Gradients of attrition tip.

Somewhere in a pause, a moment's night-time
    silence, exhaustion leans over the whole land.

We need to see the line move.
Our curiosity must be appeased.
Or we will lose interest. And what then?

The verge

The ground must still be held under the soldier's boot. The dead must still be buried.
                    A Terrible Love of War, James Hillman

The bodies lie next to each other
scarcely different.
There is only the smallest
movement now,
now earth and dust have
fallen back to earth.
One draws, just, slow
breaths.
The other is the other
side of a terribly thin line.
The line began
just now,
a handful of seconds ago.

Both have great
distances to travel.
Both will be gathered,
tended to according
to their needs. There is
tenderness and horror
for both, in both.

Cast on the field's
verge, one will discover
the earth's slow
turn, will spend
slow time

with every season.
One will rise from it,
in time, in part.

At the moment of
impact each is matter,
earth, flesh
no different to the soft loam
the farmed and tended
fields for which they fought.
One's face, the other's
hand, so nearly touching,
so thin the line
of time and soil.

The one that
breathes is deep
beneath himself, he must rise
from this long deep
slowly. He must
understand, accept
in every cell the breadth
of what has happened.
The other
has his long slow
journey too; his long leave,
his slow transfiguration,
the gathering, the slow flight
home, to lodge
discarnate, loving,
wrapped around hearts.

How they matter, these
bodies, these men,

these particular men, this
animate and precious flesh.

They will pass,
somewhere on their journeys:
the body less than
living, the body more than dead.
They will stay as well
here now
as everything stills,
hands-breadth separate
on the damp October earth.

RECKONING

Surety

We have gathered up our efforts
and accomplishments, have
made from them a den, a hide,
a sanctuary. Safe behind

their comfort we have prospered,
grown adult and astute.
But even so we can't withstand
that slide towards unease

which edges every organ dried-
blood red when some unwary
realisation backlights everything.
Bad things may come.

Years may not move forward.
They may shutter, stall,
forget themselves, become
distracted and intractable,

while out beyond the curtains
where we didn't think to look,
a feral chill may gather up
its own intent, its own inheritance.

We may buy insurance,
insulation, remedies and lies:
a life where panic
hides deeper than valuables.

We may defend our due.
But outside crawls anxiety.

Outside lies our inside, exposed
in all its vanity and debt.

Can all our clean deeds and
conscience help us now?
Stripped in a raging world
of innocence they cannot.

#Bring your true self to work

I ran from the room when the meeting ended. I had become
detached from the universal credit business case. Stepping
sideways, the air was full of crackling. It was a mistake.

Disclaimer: the rest is secret, mystical. I don't know what
the story is you tell yourself but it's a good one, right?
The air was full of crackling. People hover frozen and opaque.

You slide away, beckon the car crash to the brick wall
and just step sideways. A sudden sickening reversal.
Brick chips and disaster fly from the impact.

People hover frozen and opaque. Going down and down
and down the worst of rabbit-holes – it's a good one, right?
Disclaimer: it was not a death threat that I said to you.

On the 15th floor, elaborate fantasies of governance.
It was not a death threat that I said to you. Only a sudden
sickening reversal of flesh and breath, sliding away.

The vigilant right brain took its eye off me for moments.
It was a mistake. Disclaimer: I existed wild alone with
breath. I ran from the room when the meeting ended.

Detached from the universal credit business case,
I existed wild alone, all flesh and breath. Stepping
sideways, I beckoned the car crash to the brick wall.

The vigilant right brain took its eye off me for moments.
Brick chips and disaster fly from the impact, going
down and down and down the worst of rabbit-holes.

On the 15th floor, elaborate fantasies of governance. I don't know what the story is you tell yourself, but it's a mistake. Flesh and breath exist. The rest is secret, mystical.

Reckoning

I see that you have tried to play
the game. Have built a personality
that's adequate for work.
Well done. You have advanced
enough, achieved enough.

And now you are very tired, wishing
to tread from air-conditioned
buildings into a raw world, step
weightless through the
neurons of your whole brain.

To follow the unlit branches,
leap the electric gaps,
lie stretched in flickered fields
where rationality can rest
and nothing does or can add up.

To reach for sun on skin and find it,
sweet, familiar. To travel the spine's
length. To visit the ancient forest,
stand unvoiced and listening,
feel sensation pouring down.

Befriend it again

Go backward, backward to the bedsit.
Recall the thin bleak texture of your former life.
Time spent lying on your bed in grey mid-
morning, room hazing across like dusk.
Milk near-off near-finished on the window-sill,
not quite sufficient food for later on.
And banging on the landing, who knows who.

The void was ready, empty, always at your shoulder.
Remember how it wrapped around the bed
the day you watched paint dry.
Beneath the pier it spoke to you, and incarnated,
conjured up, walked with you through
brick-dripped archways, passages and steps,
luring you to distances and sea.

Befriend it again. This is your habitat, where
rain and shivered neon light the fire escape,
pebbles roll and rumble in your bones.
This is your consolation and your rest.
Blood is brine and warmth and nothing else.
There is loose and scouring saltedness.
A clean and burning after-freezing heat.

Room 13

Outside the window
is the iron rain-pooled fire escape,
rust streaking render,
loading bays and ventilation
fans and slammed vans.

Outside the window is
a strip of green shag carpet,
half-cans of engine oil,
quad bikes and seagulls sifting
flesh from the inedible.

Outside the window lie
remnants of old relationships,
a muffled sense of hope,
a memory of embarrassment,
the future and a dog.

This is the ragged junkyard of
reality, picked over by your
tender patient skin; a crackled
understanding fleeing precious
away over the beach.

This is noise of birds and traffic,
streetlamps on the promenade,
signals in the liquid icy air
to tempt you and follow you
over the stones.

Face it

We're in the mammal's crazy drivenness, the
gathering and gathering, the wide-eyed scan of
everything, the spooking scattered charge of
panicked fear or panicked aspiration seizing up
as circumstance repeats, persists, goes by un-
noticed unforgiven in the fragmentary grasp, in the
fragmentary weft, in the fragmentary fizzing action
of our suspended struggling scared prey self.

We're in the trampled weightiness, the swerving
certain righteousness, the shove, the gasp, the
pointless playful race, the galloping direction on
direction on direction, the exhausted fall, the
thrown bones on the soft spun surface of the earth,
horizon on horizon on horizon as the trails snake
and we tread in the gravel and the tarmac and
the grass seeking something that looks like home.

We're in the invented edifice, the palace of the mind,
living in our house of cards and walking in our
wonderful garden of dopamine, a place without
moment, place without consequence, a custom-
made cosmology fine-tuned for our diversion
where the puzzles, words and purposes all beckon
with reward, a hiding place, a holiday, a paradise
with a burning smell entering under the door.

When all else ends

In light rain
in your own flesh, sat
on the back of a park bench
feet on the wooden seat
in light rain, in 18 years
of your own self
in 18 years
in a leather jacket, hide
surrendered to you
next to your cold face
next to your cold hands
mid-afternoon
infinity, a neverness
where drops run down
the railings,
drops run down
the leather, down your
face and trace you
whispered on the bench
alive, extreme
exposed
eclipse-flashed into permanence
existing burst within the world
this
is where you'll be
when all else ends
between ages
between selves
between wonder and dismay
within the firmament
naked, in something else's skin.

FREE WILL

1

Walk backwards from the bullet entering the skull.

Walk backwards across the space, the perfect parabola.

Watch the bullet re-join the gun, heel first, and swallow the explosion and fit snug back into the case.

Relax the finger off the trigger.

Let the shoulder drop, the arm fall, the stance relax.

Let the air settle.

2

Under the skin the nerves still buzz and sparkle.
Under the skin the muscles flick and twitch.
The blood still flows, the hormones sluice and I
                         become aware of my breath.

3

The brain is talking to itself but not to me. It's fidgeting,
        and wired up, and may have misread the situation.

It seems to be testing out an alibi
        or whether I may have been provoked.

It's wondering what's the scope for changing how things were.

It's good to know my brain is on the case on my behalf
        trying to get me out of this.

But it can't locate
        a clear dark streak of purpose
        in anything that happened here today.

4

I know the things they'll ask me: questions of motivation and intent.
What were the things I thought and planned and hoped for.
What drove me out there carrying a gun.

Right now it's hard to recollect how thinking works, or memory. I'm
    reaching into space and finding nothing –

no causal chains, no hate, no hope, no narrative report

just debris from an endless
    aftershock.

My mind has shut and sulked and left me locked
    outside – not even invited to my own fate; not
    even invited to my own identity.

They'll say well did you do it? And I will have to answer:
    no one else did.

5

The universe begins and particles fly out
and over time there is alignment, coalescence,
restless patterns which emerge, collapse, emerge
and settle into something nearing constancy,
a balance tracking history and the future in the sky.
How would we be different? It was those same
matching patterns, the alignment in our lives
which put me in his way and he in mine
on an overcast damp day when earlier I noticed
snowdrops blooming by an oak tree in the park
and stopped to find them beautiful.

6

It's not the universe that did it. It's not the air the bullet pushed aside that allowed it, or the priming of the gun that takes the blame. It's not my education or my family or the overspill of synapses that race around my brain, and it's not the bad night's sleep I had last night, lying awake and fretting in the darkness over many different things.

7

Much coalesced to create the moment.

Much coalesced to create the moment when the white van
    rounded the corner across from the DIY store

when the leopard stirred on its wooden bed at London Zoo
    and licked its paw

when the puddle by the cross-road rippled and spilled into the
    drain

when I reached inside my jacket as he did too and his world
    went black while mine entered an infinite moment of
    silence and solitude.

Time does not pass lightly.

Each moment has its million wounded parents and its million
    haunted offspring.

They stain us with their certainties before they travel on.

8

The gun was in my hand,
    the drawer, the gun was in its box.
The gun was on the counter with its price tag on,
    was in a crate, a factory, a drawing board, a mind.
It was a hard clean streak of cleverness & violence & cash
    cascading through its absence, through its coming into form,
    through liberation from legality

to land with me,
who swung it up and shot the man.

9

Trace it: the bullet goes back to the gun. My fingers wrap around the grip.

There are constant quantum births and deaths but I won't dispute how matter moved today.

10

This is the small room. I think
there will be more small rooms
for me, like this one with its
moulded bed and heavy door.

I think there will be noise
for me, and interruption, and
from my body in this cell
will spill bureaucracy

my name assigned unique
identifying references, a flow
from database to database
through unfamiliar agencies.

Much will unfurl from those
few seconds on the sidewalk
by the ordinary house, the
stony garden where his blood

splashed, the tarmac
driveway where the knife
that he was holding clattered
down, while I stood still.

For him there will be hush,
and small rooms too,
white sterile places as they
say he didn't die. Like me

he'll be confined, assessed,
will be on lists, will undergo
the years of process. I have
bound the two of us together,

me and a man I barely knew.

11

I could have decided not to go out today – god knows there's been whole lifetimes when I haven't left my room. I could have been a different man, a calmer man, a man more blessed with concentration and foresight. I could have missed the crossing, missed the bus, stopped in to buy a drink, or paused to tie my lace or been distracted by a phone call from my mum. I could have travelled far more warily, been more contained and more alert, more serious, befitting someone carrying a gun. I could have figured worse things of the world and braced myself for provocation and for pain. Today I neglected to do that. I travelled in good faith and expectation and arrived to see my friends and see a girl I liked and have a barbecue, and never even made it to the front door. My acts and self and the merciless hard day washed through instead.

12

I could have wished the day had turned out different.
      But apprehended now from where I find myself
           I'm not sure how it could have done.

Movements took the precise time they did.
      They happened in the precise way they did. They
           pooled across a morning free from hurry or alarm.

My laces didn't come undone and no one called
      and every action was embedded in itself and in the air
           and in its next-door seconds and the day.

The moments were wedged crossways in eternity, secured
      in every dimension. Rattle the universe how you like,
           they won't shake loose.

I try but can't find any versions of today that don't hold
      confrontation by the dustbins, sudden scuffled shouts
           and someone falling.

13

Unearth your professional opinions.
The weeks will be abundant with commentary.

Pick your place of judgement
and what you will judge me on.

Sirens wreathe around you as you work,
playing into an intricate distance.

Events were what they are, are what they are,
have always been what they still are.

A muted headache grief that I could cry for
moves along my bones and settles in.

14

Walk backwards from the bullet entering the skull.

Walk backwards across the space, the perfect parabola.

Crank the day

        forwards or backwards or forwards or

            backwards.

Piece and unpiece it.

Count all the neurons sparkling in our heads.

See how the events that mark the day don't change.

Notes

Hackney Brook

This really happened: https://metro.co.uk/2014/11/14/your-tax-money-at-work-parliament-pays-workers-to-pick-leaves-off-trees-4948903/

Bracelet

With thanks to Lieve de Bree.

Closing focus sequence

The quotations are from *A Terrible Love of War*, a highly personal and poetic exploration of the psychology of war by James Hillman (2004, Penguin Press, New York), pp. 91, 92 and 138. The starting point for 'Closing focus' was two different AI translations of the same Russian battlefield report. 'Re/wilding' was inspired by 'Defensive Rewilding', an article by Brian Schmidt (2023, RUSI).

Acknowledgements

A number of poems in this collection, or earlier versions of them, first appeared in magazines. Thanks are due to the editors.

'Made and made over' was first published by the London Borough of Haringey as the joint winning poem in the Mayor of Enfield's Poetry Competition 2012.

'This is the truth' was first published in *Iota*.

'Rosary' was first published in *Envoi*.

'Obsidian's cousin' was first published in *Shearsman*.

'Free will' was first published in *Long Poem Magazine*.

'Re/wilding' was first published in *The Rialto*.

'Bracelet' and 'dog, woman' were first published in the anthology *Non-regulated Community Learning*, ed. Fran Lock, Culture Matters, 2025.

www.ingramcontent.com/pod-product-compliance
Ingram Content Group UK Ltd.
Pitfield, Milton Keynes, MK11 3LW, UK
UKHW022357110126
466845UK00003BA/104

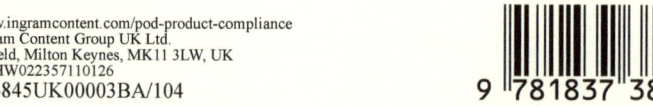